BIRTHING PROPHETIC SONS

BIRTHING PROPHETIC SONS

Understanding the training process of prophetic sons.

By Dr. John A. Tetsola

End Time Wave Publications

Birthing Prophetic Sons

Understanding the Training Process of Prophetic Sons

ISBN 1-889389-24-2

TABLE OF CONTENTS

CHAPTER 1

BIRTHING PROPHETIC SONS
IN THE SEASONS OF TRAINING

For I have no one like him— no one of so kindred a spirit—
who will be so genuinely interested in your welfare and
devoted to your interests.

For the others all seek [to advance] their own interests, not
those of Jesus Christ, the Messiah.

But Timothy's tested worth you know, how as a son with his
father he has toiled with me zealously [serving and helping
to advance] the good news (the Gospel).

I hope therefore to send him promptly, just as soon as I know
how my case is going to turn out.

Philippians 2:20-23 (AMP)

As we prepare for a new season in God, it is so imperative that the men and women that are being birthed in this hour are sons that have been reared and raised in the houses of fathers who are prophetic. These kinds of sons are what we call "prophetic sons." They are a pure breed of men and women whose ultimate purpose is to pursue and take the Voice of God to their generation and in return birth other sons.

These are protégés or sons that realize they have no access to the father unless they have consistently pursued him. They are extremely discreet regarding anything concerning or involving the mentor. This type of son will die with the secret information locked inside his heart, not letting it outside his mouth. These sons do not confuse familiarity with disrespect. This type of protégé or son understands that intimacy does not guarantee access. Respect does. They do not take access for granted. Access is privilege. It is not something that is guaranteed. Access is something that is given. These are sons who understand and value the focus of the mentor. They respect what the mentor respects when in the presence of the mentor. They do not view their right to disagree as an opportunity to disrespect the mentor or to prove their own individuality. You respect what the mentor respects when in his presence.

Pure prophetic sons are those who will be the first to defend in the storms of false accusation against their father. These are sons who will be the first to cover their father through the storms of true accusations against their father. I have cut off as quick as you can blink an eye relationships with preachers and even friends who had badmouthed my spiritual father. Now you may say that we don't need to have that kind of extreme because everybody is not going to like your mentor or agree with him. Let me tell you something. You are entitled to your own opinion about my father, but just not around me. When I am in your presence, the moment you go badmouthing the person I call my spiritual father, you and I have just separated. It is like sitting with a group of friends or preachers and all of a sudden, they start going off saying a bunch of bad, derogatory things about your wife or about your mother. Would you sit there saying "Well, you are entitled to your own opinion." No, no, no! You would be throwing dishes and plates. You would be on top of them quicker than they could cry or dial 911. Yet, for some reason, we think if God puts a spiritual father into our lives we're just supposed to let anybody and everybody just say whatever they want. That is a lie. When you are in the presence of your spiritual father, you must respect what he respects. We don't have to agree on everything right down the line. You may like purple and I may like blue. That is not a problem. But when it comes to the people that make the biggest difference in my life, I am not going to sit anywhere and let you agree to be disagreeable, or let you just vent your little two cents, no more than I would expect you to let me vent mine. You have to understand that a true protégé, a pure prophetic son, defends his father.

And when you get to defending a father in the storms of false accusation, you are going to definitely surface false friendships in your life. There are going to be some people who were your friends, who will suddenly become your enemies, because of your stand. People who don't have enough aptitude and intelligence to investigate rumors, until they find the facts or lack of facts, are people who are not worth being in a relationship with anyway. Pure prophetic sons are protégés who will cut off certain relationships with others that blatantly disregard or slander the mentor. These are sons who realize that when they become linked to the mentor, they become representatives of the mentor. They realize that every action of their conduct not only represents God, but also represents the one that God used to bring them to the place where they are. They also realize that the privilege that they have been extended by the mentor to be a representative of the mentor is something that is not only very valuable, but must be protected and respected. When your spiritual father or mentor endorses you or recommends you publicly, you are not living for yourself and ministry. You are living for the one whose recommendation and endorsement are upon you.

These are sons whose passion for the success of the father is as strong as the passion for their own. The success of the father matters a great deal to the protégé. They rejoice when the mentor is successful. Pure prophetic sons realize that they will never stop being a son. They may in the future mentor or father other people or sons, but they will always be a son to their father. Information never plateaus. It always progresses. These types of protégés or sons realize that success is not the opportunity for disconnecting, but the reason for staying connected. They realize that they may surpass the mentor in public achievement, but never in private counsel. These are sons that always serve the father. They are always very attentive and intuitive toward the every need and movement of the father. Smart sons always realized that they never stop serving their spiritual father. You can pastor a church of five thousand, but the moment the protégé or son is in the father's presence, he is still the father and the son still serves him. He carries his mentor's bags and calls for taxis. A servant always maintains a servant's heart irrespective of the success of the servant. Why does the son do that? Because that is his spiritual father. That should not come as a surprise to any of us, if we really understand the concept of spiritual fathering. The only way you are going to keep serving is if you keep respecting. If you respect your spiritual father or mentor greatly, you are going to keep serving. You don't have to take a special course on how to serve. It just flows smoothly and easily. Whenever you have problems serving, you will always find that you have problems respecting. The moment you respect something, you value it and the moment you value it, you serve it.

These are sons who will respectfully communicate information to the father and will respect the protocol of properly addressing the father when conversing. These are sons who do not attempt to teach the mentor. They understand that the tail does not wag the dog. The mentor learns from the son, but the son does not exact his knowledge on the mentor. These pure sons have a loyalty to the chief and not to the Indians. The son's loyalty is to his or her mentor. Anybody else in the mentor's life can come and go and it does not make a difference to the son. Even though he treats the people in his mentor's life with respect, his complete loyalty is to the mentor.

FATHER-SON FEAR

Do thy diligence to come shortly unto me:

For Demas hath forsaken me, having loved this present world, and is departed unto Thessalonica; Crescens to Galatia, Titus unto Dalmatia.

Only Luke is with me. Take Mark, and bring him with thee: for he is profitable to me for the ministry.

And Tychicus have I sent to Ephesus.

The cloke that I left at Troas with Carpus, when thou comest, bring with thee, and the books, but especially the parchments.

Alexander the coppersmith did me much evil: the Lord reward him according to his works:

Of whom be thou ware also; for he hath greatly withstood our words.

At my first answer no man stood with me, but all men forsook me: I pray God that it may not be laid to their charge.

Notwithstanding the Lord stood with me, and strengthened me; that by me the preaching might be fully known, and that

**all the Gentiles might hear: and I was delivered out of the
mouth of the lion.**

II Timothy 4:9-17

At times the reaction between the father and the son can
seem misunderstood to the other or even illogical. However,
such reactions and thought processes are motivated by
particular fears that both a father and a son have that can be
the reason for hesitation in sharing information and seeking
information. It is important to realize that the father's and
son's fears are different from each other because their
positions are different from each other. There are things that
the father fears and there are things that the son fears, and
they fear it for different reasons.

The fear of the father is the fear of rejection. Fathers fear
that the son will see their human flaws and disconnect from
them because of it. Fathers fear that sons will see them in a
false pretense of perfection and the first action by the father
that shows their human side or even their imperfect side will
devastate the shroud of perfection that the son has placed on
the father, thus devastating the relationship with them. It is
important to know that the words HUMAN and IMPERFECT
used to explain this particular point are not words that will

justify the fathers' right to conduct themselves in a blatant immoral or unethical way. These words are used in a context to note that a father will have blind spots too, and sometimes imperfect belief systems that govern their reactions to certain things. A son should always keep his or her focus on the positive side of the father more than the imperfection of the father. If a father is never put in a glass house, imperfect stones will not destroy it.

FEAR OF CRITICISM

Let's look at the son's fears. The son fears criticism. A son fears not being safe enough with the father to ask for the necessary advice on how they could improve something or some areas of their lives. Such fear is normally brought on in the son's life from years of trying hard to please either an unpleaseable father in the natural, or trying hard to please a certain group of people that they thought they had to be accepted by in order to be successful in life. Sometimes it is just the blatant fear of going the extra mile to be good, only to find that they were not good enough. These examples produce emotional scars that restrict us every time we think about reaching out to someone else for help. Mostly what we do to cover our fears is to try extremely hard to secretly extract information or to imitate other successful examples of what we are doing in order to maximize our chances for success and minimize our chances for criticism. It is very important for both fathers and sons to realize that a son wants approval more than success. A son is most concerned with the father's approval of his work, more than he is concerned with others' acceptance of his work. A son will forfeit thousands of dollars and dozens of opportunities in life, just by protecting themselves from being potentially hurt or offended by the direct or even critical words of someone who sees what they could do differently early in their life.

A father must always be as attentive as possible to making it easy for the son to approach the father to seek advice or input for something they are doing. Sons need affirmation for where they are, before they will feel secure enough to seek information for where they are going. A father must make a son feel safe enough to reach out for help. It is important to understand that regardless of how strong a son might be in certain areas, they will be equally fragile in others. Elijah had no problem confronting four hundred and fifty prophets of Baal. He had no problem making fun of them, saying build your trenches bigger and then pour in more water, and then calling on the God of fire to consume their sacrifice. They all turned on one another. Then he took them to a place and he killed them all. But what did he do after that? In I Kings 18, he ran like a little boy the moment a woman named Jezebel intimidated him. He went and hid under the juniper tree and asked God to kill him. The greatest thing a father or a spiritual father can do for you, his son or his son, is to make it safe for the son to ask for advice or help. How? By not criticizing the son when he is doing something the wrong way. Also, the spiritual father must not belittle the simplicity of the questions of the son simply because he is the father.

FEAR OF SEPERATIONS

Spiritual fathers fear separation. A father feels that a son will become extremely close to him and then will become unexplainably disconnected from him. A father knows that a son's separation does not mean the end of life for either the father or the son. However, there is a bonding that is involved, even for the father, that is equivalent to the relational bond between a parent and a child. The Apostle Paul in writing to his spiritual son Timothy from prison in II Timothy 4:9-17 explained to Timothy how Demas had forsaken him and he urged Timothy to come quickly to him and to bring again John Mark. Fathers fear separation. The main reason why fathers fear separation is because they fear attachment. Fathers enjoy bonding to the son as a result of the son's pursuit. However, the father sometimes walks around with insecurity, fearing that the son may stop pursuing. Both fathers and sons feed greatly off of the spiritual and emotional energy that takes place because of the consistent impartation motivated by the consistent pursuit between. Sons, on the other hand, fear failure. The sons fear not being able to live up to the expectations of their status with the father. They fear letting the father down in certain areas and never being fully trusted again by that father. A son fears doing something unintentional that will place a stain on the relationship well into the future. Even though the fear of failing the father should never be as great as the fear of failing God, the son still knows that the approval of the father means a great deal to them and the responsibility of effectively representing the father's endorsement of them is a great duty in their life.

To whom much is given, much is required. A son fears being controlled and manipulated by the father. They fear that the father is not going to see where they really are and where they really are going. A son fears that the father does not really have his best interests at heart and that the father only wants to use the son for his own benefit and gain. If you can see and understand these fears, it will help you understand your father and it will help you understand your son. And if you can expose these fears, it can no longer grip you or hold you down.

CHAPTER 2

HOW TO RECEIVE THE TRANSFERENCE OF PROPHETIC MANTLES

Throughout history, the question regarding one of the most dramatic departures of a man of God, and the dramatic beginnings of his successor, has shared incredible insight and revelation on how the mantle could not only be transferred from one to another, but could be doubled in its impact during the transfer. Many believe the double portion of Elijah's anointing that Elisha received was, in fact, the reason why a protégé like Elisha would even pursue his mentor up to the point of his departure. However, as the Scriptures reveal to us, the double portion anointing was the result of Elisha's pursuit and not the reason he pursued. There is a reward, not just in heaven but here on earth as well, for those protégés who know that God has linked them to a mentor and stayed faithful to their mentor, even through times of adversity.

How did Elisha get the mantle of his mentor? I can tell you how he did *not* get it. He did not get it in a prayer line. He got it in the following ways. First, he burned his plow. He sowed his present to reap his future. He believed enough in his future to sow his present to get it. Those that do not sow in their present are those who are comfortable enough with it never to move on, or they are those who don't believe that they have a future. He sowed his personal plans to reap his spiritual assignment. He realized that his present was a seed and not a harvest. He realized that he could not reap from something that he did not sow into. He qualified for a double portion seed. You can never take the plows of your present into the promised land of your future. He realized that if he kept what he had, it would be all that he ever had. If he let go of what he had, it would be the beginning of all that he would ever receive. He realized that seed was not just an offering of choice. It was a weapon for movement. He realized that when something left his present, it went into his future and prepared his future for his arrival there. God's calling upon his life became his obsession more than his profession. A calling unpursued is a calling unfulfilled.

And the sons of the prophets that were at Jericho came to Elisha, and said unto him, Knowest thou that the LORD will take away thy master from thy head to day? And he answered, Yea, I know it; hold ye your peace.

II Kings 2:5

The second way he got his father's mantle was by disconnecting from what others thought in order to follow what he knew. He understood the relationship of focus to one's destination. What you look at the longest will either pull you through or pull you down. He understood that he was not required to defend where he was going to those that were not going there. People that are for you will either go with you or help you get there. But people who are not for you will just have to watch you get there. He understood that the moment you open up the door to opinions, focus walks out. The more you listen to the opinions of those not going where you are going, the more your focus will become diluted, and the more you become double minded about your destination. He understood that the end result of his assignment would be determined by whether or not he would allow God to promote it or a person to distract it. People that are for you will impact your focus. People that are not for you will distract your focus. He understood that the seed which he had sown to follow a man of God would not bring a harvest if he was too quiet. He understood that even if he was wrong for pursuing a man of God, he knew that any attempt to obey God would not go unrewarded.

> **And it came to pass, when they were gone over, that Elijah said unto Elisha, Ask what I shall do for thee, before I be taken away from thee. And Elisha said, I pray thee, let a double portion of thy spirit be upon me.**

> **And he said, Thou hast asked a hard thing: nevertheless, if thou see me when I am taken from thee, it shall be so unto thee; but if not, it shall not be so.**

> **II Kings 2:9-10**

Third, he received the double portion by following his father without the guarantee of what he would receive as a result of his pursuit. He realized that he could not be destined for greatness unless he was connected to greatness. He realized that the significant seed that he sowed to follow a man of God had to be sowed in faith believing that God was ordaining his future, even when Elisha could not see his future. He was willing to pursue something that he did not know the end result of. Obedience is going to require you to follow an instruction without an explanation. God is going to tell you to stretch forth your rod, but He is not going to tell you whether the water is going to part. God is going to tell you not to bow before Nebuchadnezzar, but He is not going to tell you if there will be a fourth man in the fire. You must have faith in the God of the instructions, even when your logic can't explain it. He understood that every time God gives you present instructions, He has a future destination on His mind. God never instructs you because of where you are, but because of where you are going.

> **And it came to pass, when the LORD would take up Elijah into heaven by a whirlwind, that Elijah went with Elisha from Gilgal.**
>
> **And Elijah said unto Elisha, Tarry here, I pray thee; for the LORD hath sent me to Bethel. And Elisha said unto him, As the LORD liveth, and as thy soul liveth, I will not leave thee. So they went down to Bethel.**
>
> **II Kings 2:1-2**

Fourth, Elisha received his mentor's mantle because he knew the power of pursuit. Elisha realized that if he was not willing to pursue, he was not willing to possess. Reckless abandonment determines realistic achievement. He realized that pursuit is the last stage before possession. He realized that possession is for the hungry and not for the haughty. He realized that pursuit would require him to take a step with nothing. He realized that pursuit begins with his desire and not another's permission. You will never possess anything until the pursuit of going after it overwhelms the passivity of living without it. He realized that pursuit requires more focus than ability. He realized that present pursuit would require him to move through memories of past failures. He realized that present pursuit would require him to pursue through the rejection of his mentor. He realized that present pursuit would require him to pursue through the natural insecurity of no guarantee of what he would receive as a result of his pursuit. They offer opportunities. You must get this in your spirit. He realized that present pursuit would require him to pursue something that he did not know existed.

Nobody knew the double portion existed until they got to the top of the mountain and Elisha said give me double of what you have. He realized that if you want something that you have never had, you have to do something that you have never done. Pursuit silences regret from creating a photograph of what you could have had as you pursued. The double portion cannot be trusted to complacent people. People who are not changing the world are only complaining about it. That is how Elisha got his double portion.

ABORTING THE MANTLE OF THE FATHER

How do you abort a double portion anointing? By sowing your Isaac future in an Ishmael soil. Part of the reason that makes Ishmael soil cursed soil is that it is cursed. This means that it was something that God did not ordain and God cannot bless. A soil that is not good to build a foundation on will not be good enough to build a structure upon.

Second, wrong timing. This means that God could not build right vision at the wrong time. Wrong places perpetuate wrong focus. Wrong places are where wrong people hang out. It could even be the wrong place. God cannot bless you in some places that you are not supposed to be. That seed that is sown in the wrong soil cannot produce a blessed harvest. The longer you stay in a wrong place, the longer you will live in wrong pain. Right pictures do not fit in wrong frames. Every time you are in the wrong place, you access the wrong people. The right people cannot come into your life in the wrong place. The longer you stay with the wrong people, the longer you delay God in connecting you to the right ones.

FINDING YOUR FATHER

How do you find your spiritual father or mentor? First,

allow God to link you, more than you try to link yourself. Don't let your heart's desire for a mentor or father spoil God's maneuvering to link you to one. The manipulation of head logic is always the enemy to the determination of heart desire. Allow time to work for you. Impatience is the only reason you will become linked with the wrong people and pursue wrong opportunities. Go with your heart. Find the right people that God is linking you to and allow them to speak into your life.

Silence the voice of qualification. God does not call the qualified. He qualifies the called. Don't allow your enemy to depress you out of your future, based on what you believe you are capable of.

MAINTAINING THE FATHER-SON RELATIONSHIP

First, keep pursuing, Pursuit is permanent, not momentary. Your level of pursuit will determine your level of credibility and credibility determines promotion. The relationship with your mentor will require you to go where the mentor is, more than waiting for the mentor to come to you. A mentor will not chase you to teach you what they know. You will have to chase the mentor to find out what they know. You will never be able to chase the mentor out of convenience.

Second, keep learning. The quality of the father's information is determined by the quality of the son's questions. Don't be afraid to interrogate something that you don't understand. Don't be as concerned with impressing the mentor with your ability as you are with asking the mentor for help. Smart protégés or sons are more concerned with sustaining success, than they are with achieving success. Success is harder to keep than it is to reap.

Third, keep serving. The father in the Lord that God links you to never stops being your father. Ministering to your mentor positions you in the flow of God's favor. Before you can be a great successor, you must become a great server.

Finally, keep sowing. The more consistent you seed into the soil of your mentor, the more intensively you will reap the mantle of your mentor. When God gives you a spiritual father, He did not just give you someone who can teach you, he gave you someone with a mantle of blessing on their life that you can sow into, so that you can increase in blessings. The soil of a God-ordained mentor is some of the most fertile soil you will ever sow into. Smart protégés are protégés who realize that the more successful they become, the more dependent they become on a mentor in order to handle the success. When you keep serving, keep sowing, keep pursuing and keep learning, God is going to link you to the right people who will be instrumental in helping you birth destiny.

CHAPTER 3

RAISING AND TRAINING
PROPHETIC CHILDREN

Verily I say unto you, Whosoever shall not receive the kingdom of God as a little child, he shall not enter therein.

Mark 10:15

And it shall come to pass in the last days, saith God, I will pour out of my Spirit upon all flesh: and your sons and your daughters shall prophesy, and your young men shall see visions, and your old men shall dream dreams:

Acts 2:17

God is not above speaking to us through the agency of a child. It is not unreasonable to expect that God would use small children to accurately communicate with His adult children. There are thousands of unsuspecting parents who have spiritually gifted children. I entreat these parents to cultivate a sensitivity to the Spirit of God within their children. The spiritual potential that lies within their souls may one day surprise you and could easily serve to protect you. Their strange dreams and childlike perceptions may seem insignificant at first, but in many instances these children are prophetic in nature. If the gift that lies within them is nurtured, God may eventually commission a prophet from within your own family.

DEVELOPING THE PROPHETIC
ANOINTING IN YOUR CHILDREN

And, ye fathers, provoke not your children to wrath: but bring them up in the nurture and admonition of the Lord.

Ephesians 6:4

How do we begin to develop the prophetic gifts that are resident within our children? The answer is fourfold. The first thing to do is to "bring them up in the nurture and admonition of the Lord." Second, our lives could some day depend on a word from a prophetic child. Third, Exodus 19:6 informs us that God has called them to be a kingdom of priests to our succeeding generations. Finally, Jesus declared "out of the mouth of babes and sucklings thou hast perfected praise" (Matthew 21:16).

METHODS OF NURTURING THE PROPHETIC

There are several methods that we must employ to nurture the prophetic within our children.

(1) Teach your children that God wishes to speak to them, even as children.

(2) Read Scriptures to your children and tell them Bible stories pertaining to the prophetic.

(3) Lay hands on your children daily, if possible. Pray for the prophetic gift to be stirred within them.

(4) Speak prophetically to your child's spirit, prophesying God's intent for him or her (Joel 2:28).

(5) Encourage your children to share even their simplest dreams or perceptions with you.

(6) Teach your children to interpret their dreams within the context of Scripture and with its symbolic implications.

(7) When possible, expose your children to valid prophetic ministry. Exposing your children to valid prophetic ministry cannot be overemphasized. Although sound biblical instruction is vital, we must remember that more is caught than taught. Therefore, to fulfill God's mandate to raise up a prophetic generation in the fear and admonition of the Lord, we must not only teach them about the prophetic, but also model it in front of them.

CHAPTER 4

THE CONFLICT BETWEEN PROPHETIC SHEEP AND PASTORAL LEADERSHIP

The relationship of the prophetic ministry and the church must be fully understood. Conflict between prophetic sheep and pastoral leadership exists, and only deliberate ignorance would prevent anyone from admitting that a serious breach has developed between these two groups. The breach is so great that most prophetic people avoid pastors as though they had the plague. Likewise, most pastors are relieved when prophetic people leave their churches.

Why has this misunderstanding festered into an almost incurable wound? On one hand, the pastor feels offended because the prophetic person is reluctant to come under church authority. On the other side, the prophetic person feels threatened by harsh treatment, which he interprets as a pastor's over-controlling abuse of authority. The result produces a relational stand-off. As an apostle and a prophet, I understand the inner fears of both sides. For the pastor who is committed to Scriptural balance, moderation, local body life and biblical submission, it is extremely hard to embrace a prophetic person who seems to be mystical, free-spirited, independent and extreme in the area of revelation.

The prophetic person feels an obligation to protect his ministry and gifting. Because of this effort to protect, it is equally hard to submit himself or his gift to the jurisdiction of pastoral oversight. This is most especially true if the pastor appears to be intolerant, unapproachable and skeptical of the prophetic. The result is that both feel rejected by the other, making it difficult to maintain a working relationship.

THE MARRIAGE OF THE
PROPHETIC AND THE PASTORAL

In order to understand the relationship that both pastoral ministry and the prophetic share and in order to rectify the misunderstanding, there must first be an understanding of the roles played by each party. The prophetic person must understand the dynamics of pastoral function and the pastor must understand the dynamics of the prophetic. Most important, both must recognize the role of the other as vital to the church.

In order to define the prophetic ministry and its relationship to the church, let's look at some of the things we said earlier in this book. Let us divide the prophetic into four basic levels. The first level is the *spirit of prophecy*, second is the *gift of prophecy*, third is the *prophetic mantle*, and finally, fourth is the *office of the prophet*. The first level, which is the spirit of prophecy, is the most common form of prophetic utterance in the church. According to Revelation 19:10, this manifestation of prophecy is the same as the testimony of Jesus Christ. In specific terms, it is an anointing of the Holy Spirit that enables people who are not prophets or who do not possess a prophetic gift to prophesy. When this form of prophetic anointing falls upon a group of people, even backsliders have been known to prophesy with great inspiration (I Samuel 19:20-23).

The gift of prophecy, on the other hand, unlike the spirit of prophecy is limited to a fewer number of people. It is one of the nine gifts of the Spirit found in I Corinthians 12 and is given by the Spirit "to whomever he wills." This gift is a resident gift and can be utilized at any time by those who are developed in their gifting (Acts 21:8-11).

> **So he departed thence, and found Elisha the son of Shaphat, who was plowing with twelve yoke of oxen before him, and he with the twelfth: and Elijah passed by him, and cast his mantle upon him.**
>
> **I Kings 19:19**

> **And when the sons of the prophets which were to view at Jericho saw him, they said, The spirit of Elijah doth rest on Elisha. And they came to meet him, and bowed themselves to the ground before him.**
>
> **II Kings 2:15**

The next is the prophetic mantle. It is a ministry function empowered by a strong prophetic anointing that rests upon an individual at all times. It far exceeds the first two levels that we discussed in commitment and calling. In commitment, it requires a lifestyle devoted to the prophetic. In calling, it is often preparatory for those who will later function as mature prophets. This prophetic mantle can fall upon a person who is in close association with a prophet or group of prophets.

And are built upon the foundation of the apostles and prophets, Jesus Christ himself being the chief corner stone;

Ephesians 2:20

And he gave some, apostles; and some, prophets; and some, evangelists; and some, pastors and teachers;

For the perfecting of the saints, for the work of the ministry, for the edifying of the body of Christ:

Ephesians 4:11-12

And God hath set some in the church, first apostles, secondarily prophets, thirdly teachers, after that miracles, then gifts of healings, helps, governments, diversities of tongues.

I Corinthians 12:28

The final level is the office of the prophet. It is the highest realm of the prophetic. To possess this office, one is required to have a sovereign calling, extensive training and multiple encounters with the presence of God. The prophet here operates in a governmental office, directing and correcting the church. He lives and operates in a realm of forth-telling, rebuke, affirmation, revelation, illumination, divine utterance, prediction, encouragement, dreams, visions, exhortation, correction and ministry confirmation. It is important to understand that just because you operate with a gift of prophecy, that does not make you a prophet. Only the one called as a prophet has the latitude and the authority to direct and correct the Body of Christ.

PROPHETS RELATING TO AUTHORITY

When Jesus was asked to come and heal the servant of a certain centurion, the centurion said to Jesus:

"Sir, don't inconvenience yourself by coming to my home, for I am not worthy of any such honor or even to come meet you. Just speak a word from where you are, and my servant boy will be healed! I know, because I am under authority of my superior officers, and I have authority over my men. I only need to say 'Go!' and they go; or 'Come!' and they come; and to my slave, 'Do this or that,' and he does it. So just say, 'Be healed!' and my servant will be well again!"

Luke 7:7-8 (TLB)

When you are responsible for someone, you must also be responsible to someone. To have authority, you must also be under authority. The same applies to any person or ministry in today's church. Whether a believer is a pastor or prophet, church secretary or worship leader, all who labor in the Lord must defer to a higher authority than themselves. This act of submission places the believer in a flow of divine order. Although many Christians wrestle with the issue of submission, God's order of authority is clear. First, we must submit to God. Next, we must submit to those whom God has placed over us. Finally, we must show an attitude of submission toward our peers. Scripture describes this as "submitting yourselves one to another in the fear of God" (Ephesians 5:21).

PROPHETS AND SUBMISSION

As they ministered to the Lord, and fasted, the Holy Ghost said, Separate me Barnabas and Saul for the work whereunto I have called them.

Acts 13:2

Then pleased it the apostles and elders, with the whole church, to send chosen men of their own company to Antioch with Paul and Barnabas; namely, Judas surnamed Barsabas, and Silas, chief men among the brethren:

Acts 15:22

No man is an island to himself. If we believe this is true, then all Christians are part of the larger picture. For those who are prophetic, this bigger picture is the local church. In the same way that the New Testament prophets were church based, prophetic people must also be accountable to the authority structure God has established. Without this connection, we are in danger of becoming isolated Lone Rangers and will act like renegade prophets who answer to no one but themselves. This applies to all levels of prophetic ministry.

In the church today, submission and authority have become nasty language for most believers. With the awareness of the prophetic, there is even greater contention over to whom the prophet should submit. A number of Christians believe the prophet is autonomous and answers to no one but God. Some say that the prophet must be under the authority of a seasoned apostle. Others declare that the prophet's ministry is subordinate to the pastor of the church where he attends or ministers.

The prophet should submit to the pastor he frequently relates to, such as the pastor of the church where he is based, or a pastor to whom he is connected in a covenant relationship. Also, when ministering in a local church setting, the prophet must submit his ministry to the pastor of that church. From the time he enters the church meeting until he leaves, the prophet must be sensitive to the pastor's authority over that congregation. Unless the pastor fully releases his governmental right to the prophet, the prophet is limited in doing only that which is allowed by the pastor. If the prophet attempts to minister contrary to the limitations set by the pastor, he is in direct violation of spiritual authority. The prophet has two choices. He can choose to submit himself to the wishes of that particular pastor, or he can go to another church where he is fully accepted and released to minister.

THE PASTORAL STRENGTH IN THE LOCAL CHURCH

The position that a pastor holds in his church is much like the position held by the head of a household. Both have the authority to regulate, to establish protocol and to set boundaries, etc. Which of you will enter a man's house and attempt to do as you please? None, I am sure. If the head of the house requested that you take off your shoes before entering, then out of respect you would comply. If he said dinner would be served at five o'clock, then you would come to the table at five, not six. The rules might seem unnecessary or even silly, nonetheless they are the rules of that house.

Right or wrong, he is the head of his home and deserves respect from those who enter into his sphere of influence.

The same is true of a church and its pastor. While in his sanctuary, you come under his authority. If the pastor doesn't want you to lay hands on people, then don't lay hands on people. When he restricts you from prophesying, then don't prophesy. If he gives you 30 minutes to speak, then take 30 and not 40. Remember, it is always better to submit to godly authority than to undermine authority.

Finally, if you feel that as a prophet you cannot comply with the rules, then don't hang around to complain or cause trouble. Instead, go privately to the pastor and kindly inform him that under the present circumstances you are unable to return and minister prophetically in his church. Then ask God to lead you to a church that is more compatible with your ministry. Pray that you will be hooked up with a pastor who understands your prophetic ministry and is sympathetic to your methods, doctrine and ministry life.

The same principle applies to those who have a prophetic gift or prophetic mantle. If your church doesn't encourage prophetic ministry, don't push the issue. Either stay and pray that God will change things or speak with the pastor and ask his blessing to find another church more favorable to the prophetic. Whatever the decision, remember to keep a good attitude.

THE PROPHETIC METRON

But we will not boast of things without our measure, but according to the measure of the rule which God hath distributed to us, a measure to reach even unto you.

For we stretch not ourselves beyond our measure, as though we reached not unto you: for we are come as far as to you also in preaching the gospel of Christ:

II Corinthians 10:13-14

METRON is the Greek word for "measure." It means "portion or degree." In this instance of Scripture it refers to the apostle's rule, but it can also be applied to a prophet's degree of rule, domain or authority. In any case, the word METRON can be used in a positive sense to reveal the measure of one's authority. In a negative sense, it can also reveal the limitations of that authority.

There are two different metrons of a prophet's rule. One is local rule. The other is the national or global rule. A prophet who has been given local rule is one who has authority in a church or churches within his city. His realm of influence is limited to a local level. He works in concert with others to build up the city church.

The national or global prophet is called to the church at large, and like the Apostle Paul, he travels from city to city in an attempt to encourage and strengthen the corporate Body of Christ. His vision is broader, his authority is weightier, his anointing is usually different than that of the local prophet. He too is submitted to eldership. Nevertheless, he has more of a pioneering spirit which enables him to move from region to region. His metron is only limited by an occasional restriction of the Holy Spirit, such as Paul experienced when he attempted to go into Asia (Acts 16:4-6).

BEING OUT OF YOUR METRON

Most contemporary prophets believe that their metron stretches as far as their airplane tickets. At times, this may be true for national and global prophets, but for local prophets it is dangerous to go where you have not been called. Any attempt to minister in an area that you have not been graced or equipped for can subject you to the attack of territorial spirits in that region. You could be hit with great temptation, physical and mental fatigue, depression, sickness or even death. If you are a local prophet, stay home and support the pastors in your city. Give your attention to the building up of the local church. Focus on the needs around you, not the needs around the world. If you are a national or global prophet, then establish a network of relationships with elders of various regions. Make sure that you work in harmony with God's global purpose for the whole Body of Christ.

PASTORAL PROPHETS

A new breed of ministers will emerge at the beginning of the year 2000. They started emerging in the middle of the 90s, but the maturity and the conspicuousness of these ministries will become more visible in the year 2000. More of these ministers will be pastors who are also prophets pastoring churches. This phenomenon may be short lived, but for a time the church will have to submit to it as an unprecedented work of the Holy Spirit.

To request a complete catalog featuring books, video or audio tapes by Dr. John A. Tetsola, or to contact him for speaking engagements, please write or call:

Ecclesia Word Ministries International
P.O. Box 743
Bronx, New York 10462

(718) 904-8530
(718) 904-8107 fax
www.ecclesiaword.org
www.reformersministries.org
email: reformers@msn.com